SEARCHING FOR ALIEN LIFE

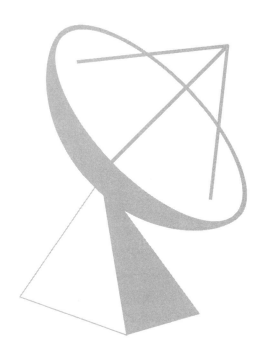

Is Anyone
Out
There?

Dennis
Brindell
Fradin

Twenty-First Century Books
Brookfield, Connecticut

Twenty-First Century Books
A Division of The Millbrook Press
2 Old New Milford Road
Brookfield, CT 06804

Library of Congress Cataloging-in-Publication Data
Fradin, Dennis Brindell
Searching for alien life : is anyone out there? / Dennis Fradin.
p.   cm.
Includes bibliographical references and index.
Summary: Examines the history of our beliefs regarding
extraterrestrial life and our continuing efforts to explore outer space.
ISBN 0-8050-4573-2
1. Life on other planets—Juvenile literature. [1. Life on other planets.
2. Outer space—Exploration.] I. Title.
QB54.F85   1997   97-12794
576.8'39—dc21   CIP
                                                  AC

Printed in the United States of America

  2 3 4 5 6 7 8 9 10

Photo Credits

pp. 10, 11, 13, 29: Corbis-Bettmann; p. 15: Rod Taylor/Archive Photos; p. 17 (both): UPI/Corbis-Bettmann; pp. 18, 20, 22 (both), 24 (both), 25, 36, 39, 71: NASA; p. 31: Geoffrey Marcy; p. 32: Lynette R. Cook; p. 41: Gilles Bouquillon/Gamma Liaison; p. 49 (left): David Dorn/J. Allen Hynek Center for UFO Studies; p. 49 (right): J. Allen Hynek Center for UFO Studies; p. 52: Dennis Bickle/J. Allen Hynek Center for UFO Studies; p. 58: Stock Montage, Inc.; p. 59: William C. Blizzard/Uniphoto Picture Agency; p. 62: Philip E. Barnhart/North American Astrophysical Observatory; p. 64: Ohio State University Radio Observatory; p. 65: Dr. Seth Shostak/SPL/Photo Researchers; p. 67: Greg Pease/Tony Stone Images

For my cousins, Paul Brindel and
Noah Bonham Brindel, with love

Acknowledgments

For their help in preparing this book, the author thanks:

Walter H. Andrus, Jr., International Director, Mutual UFO Network

Dr. Mike Davis, Senior Research Associate, Arecibo Observatory

Dr. Robert S. Dixon, Director, SETI Project, Ohio State University's "Big Ear" Radio Telescope

Bettie Greber, Executive Director, Space Studies Institute

Douglas Isbell, Public Affairs Officer, NASA

Charles Kowal, Operations Astronomer, Space Telescope Science Institute

Dr. Mark Littmann, Journalism and Astronomy Departments, University of Tennessee at Knoxville

Dr. Conley Powell, Aerospace Engineer, Teledyne Brown Engineering

Andrea Pritchard, Editor, *Alien Discussions*

Mark Rodeghier, Scientific Director, J. Allen Hynek Center for UFO Studies

Don Savage, Public Affairs Officer, NASA

Seth Shostak, Astronomer, the SETI Institute

Dr. John Stansberry, Planetary Scientist, Lowell Observatory

Dr. Jill Tarter, Director, Project Phoenix

Clyde Tombaugh, Discoverer of the planet Pluto

Dr. Tom Van Flandern, Astronomer, University of Maryland at College Park

Dr. Daniel P. Whitmire, Professor of Physics, University of Louisiana at Lafayette

Dr. Alex Wolszczan, Astronomy Department, Penn State University

A special thank-you to Judith Bloom Fradin, research assistant

Contents

1   An Age-Old Question   9

2   Exploring Our Solar System   16

3   Solar Systems Beyond   26

4   Off to the Stars!   35

5   Extraterrestrial Visitors?   47

6   *Long*-Distance Conversations With ETs   56

7   What If . . . ?   69

     Numbers, Measures, and Conversions   74

     For Further Information   76

     Index   78

1

An Age-Old Question

Scientists . . . today began a bold new experiment . . . to find out if there is life somewhere, anywhere else in the universe. . . . In a small town outside Boston, scientists today powered up this 84-foot radio telescope with two billion channels, the most powerful listening device on Earth. . . . The goal of the $250 million project is to answer the question: Are we alone in the universe, or is there life out there?

—NBC NIGHTLY NEWS, *OCTOBER 30, 1995*

On the eve of Halloween 1995, the nation's nightly newscasts described the start-up of a project that sounded like something out of a science-fiction movie. The reports about Project BETA (*B*illion-*C*hannel *E*xtraterrestrial *A*ssay) were no Halloween trick, however. Directed by Harvard University physicist Dr. Paul Horowitz, BETA employs a large radio telescope linked to a receiving system that can scan 2 billion channels in search of a message from a distant civilization. Dr. Horowitz and the other scientists involved in BETA hope it will one day discover that we are not alone in the universe.

THE INTRIGUE OF SPACE

Human beings have wondered if anyone else is out there ever since we first looked up at the night sky. One of the first people who attempted to do anything about it was said to have been Wan Hu of China. According to legend, Wan built

An ancient "spacecraft" designed by Wan-Hu of China

a "spaceship" consisting of two kites attached to a rope. His assistants lit about 50 firecrackers that were intended to propel the craft, and off went the would-be astronaut with a big bang. Wan's fate is unknown, but he certainly didn't get very far and may have landed in several pieces.

The Greek astronomer Hipparchus proved that it was impossible to fly to another heavenly body on a kite or other simple device. About 2,100 years ago, Hipparchus learned that Earth's nearest neighbor in space, the Moon, is about 250,000 miles (400,000 kilometers) away. For the next 20 centuries, people could only imagine what trips to other worlds might be like through what we call science-fiction stories.

About 1,800 years ago the Greek author Lucian wrote one of the first tales about a space voyage. Lucian's hero is sailing in a boat when a waterspout suddenly lifts it to the Moon. The reluctant space traveler discovers that the closest heavenly body to Earth is inhabited by the souls of dead people.

By the 1600s several prominent authors were concocting stories about extraterrestrials (beings from beyond Earth), or ETs. They included Cyrano de Bergerac, a French writer who is best remembered for his sword-fighting ability and his enormous nose. One of Cyrano's fictional heroes builds a flying chariot powered by firecrackers. Unlike Wan Hu, Cyrano's astronaut reaches the Moon, where strange creatures consider him a freak and lock him in a cage. In *The Dream,* by German astronomer Johannes Kepler, the travelers cross space over a bridge that appears during an eclipse. Once on the Moon, they encounter monsters that look like a combination of birds and snakes.

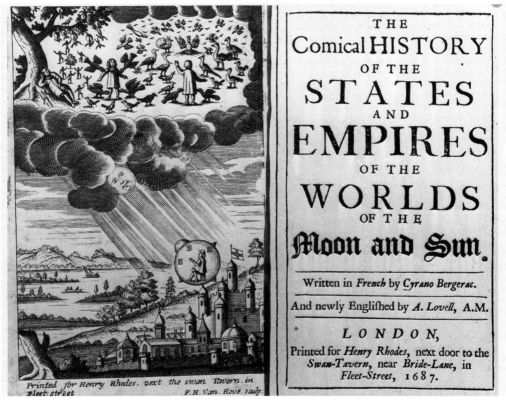

Cyrano de Bergerac (1619–1655) was a French author and soldier. He wrote plays, but he is also remembered for two science-fiction works published after his death. In these, he described various forms of space travel.

More than a century later, in 1752, the French philosopher Voltaire wrote *Micromégas*, the first story about alien visitors to Earth. Its characters include giant extraterrestrials from the planet Saturn and from a distant star.

FACT AND FICTION

Meanwhile, astronomers were learning how the universe, also called the cosmos, is constructed. Nicolaus Copernicus (1473–1543) of Poland overthrew the ancient notion that our Earth is the center of the universe. Copernicus showed that the heavenly bodies only seem to circle overhead because Earth is spinning.

Galileo Galilei (1564–1642) of Italy aimed a new invention called the telescope at the night sky and discovered that the whitish band of light called the Milky Way is composed of stars "so numerous as to be almost beyond belief." One autumn day in 1666, so the story goes, Isaac Newton (1642 1727) was sitting in an orchard when he saw an apple drop from a tree. In a flash, the English scientist realized that the same force that pulled the apple to the ground also held the Moon in orbit around the Earth and the planets in orbit around the Sun. This force was named gravitation, commonly known as gravity.

Thanks to Copernicus, Galileo, Newton, and several other scientists, by the year 1700 astronomers knew the basic facts about the universe. Scattered through space are trillions of huge balls of hot glowing gas called stars. Our Sun is a star, and it looks so large only because it is much closer to us than other stars. Around the Sun orbit several planets and their moons, all part of the Sun's family of objects known as the solar system. Outward from the Sun, the six planets known since ancient times are Mercury, Venus, Earth, Mars, Jupiter, and Saturn. The number of planets rose to nine after the discovery of Uranus in 1781, Neptune in 1846, and Pluto in 1930.

As people learned how the universe works, they began to suspect that extraterrestrials must be common, for if Earth occupies no special place and has intelligent life, why shouldn't the same be true of other worlds? The English astronomer William Herschel, who discovered Uranus, believed that various creatures lived on all the planets and even asserted that "the Sun is richly stored with inhabitants."

This painting shows the English poet John Milton looking through Galileo's telescope as Galileo teaches him about its use.

By 1881, when the Sun's surface temperature was found to be 10,000°F (5,500°C), scientists realized that stars are much too hot to support life. Around the same time, larger telescopes revealed the Moon to be bleak and seemingly lifeless. It became apparent that if extraterrestrials existed, the planets were the likeliest places where they would live.

There was a popular view in the late 1800s and early 1900s that Venus and Mars were home to intelligent life. Venus was nicknamed "Earth's Twin" because of its similarity to our own planet in size. The belief spread that beneath the clouds obscuring its surface, Venus resembled the Earth of millions of years ago and might be home to dinosaurs or even lizardlike humans.

The "Red Planet," Mars, was considered an even likelier abode of life. During the 1870s, the Italian astronomer Giovanni Schiaparelli reported seeing lines crisscrossing Mars. In 1894, Percival Lowell opened Lowell Observatory in Arizona to make intensive studies of the Red Planet. Lowell agreed with Schiaparelli that a network of lines crossed Mars and also claimed that there were dark spots scattered across the planet. Lowell formulated a theory that gained immense popularity: Just as Venus resembled the Earth of long ago, he claimed, Mars was like the Earth of the future—a dying world with a severe water shortage. To solve this problem, the Martians had constructed canals (the thin lines) through which they pumped water to their cities (the dark spots). Since building a complex canal network required intelligence and cooperation, the Martians could teach us the secret of global peace—if only we could contact them.

Schemes were hatched for informing the Martians of our presence. One idea was to plant huge wheat fields or forests in the shape of squares and triangles, in the hope that Martian astronomers would see them through their telescopes. Another plan was to build gigantic mirrors and use them to flash signals by reflected sunlight. An even more far-fetched suggestion was to dig canals in the Sahara Desert, fill them with kerosene, and set them ablaze at night. During a close approach of Mars in 1924, astronomer David Todd recommended that the world's radio stations close down for a few minutes so that we could listen to Martian radio broadcasts.

Most of the plans for communicating with Mars were never tried and none succeeded, yet occasionally there was a false alarm. Guglielmo Marconi, who invented the radio in 1895, detected some unusual radio signals during the 1920s. At first he suspected that they were messages from Martians, but they proved to be "whistlers"—a phenomenon produced by distant lightning.

Unlike Percival Lowell, science-fiction writers of the times generally portrayed Martians as evil invaders eager to kill or enslave us. On October 30, 1938, a dramatization of H. G. Wells's novel *The War of the Worlds* was presented on radio. Many listeners missed the program's introduction, which made it clear that the broadcast was fictitious. Thousands of people mistakenly believed that Martians were actually attacking Earthlings with their "heat-ray," and jumped into their cars and fled. Some were so terrified that they had to be hospitalized.

The movie The Time Machine *was based on a science-fiction novel by H. G. Wells (1866–1946). The time machine shown here was Hollywood's idea of how it looked.*

By the 1950s, movies about aliens had become the rage. The films, which had such titles as *Invaders from Mars* and *Twenty Million Miles to Earth,* seem tame by today's standards, but in their time they had Saturday-afternoon theater audiences screaming. There were also comic books and TV shows about extraterrestrials, and school science fairs usually featured someone with an exhibit about life on Mars.

As long as we couldn't go there to investigate, it seemed safe to assume that Mars and perhaps other planets were inhabited. But then came a development that allowed us to discover whether Martians, Venusians, and other creatures from the distant reaches of the solar system really exist.

2

Exploring Our
Solar System

Exploring Mars will be an exciting opportunity for the next generation. Whether Mars has life is still an open question, because the Viking *missions studied just a tiny portion of the planet's surface. We may also dig up fossils on Mars, proving that, even if none is there today, life once existed on the planet.*

—DR. MIKE DAVIS, ARECIBO OBSERVATORY (1995)

In 1919, when he published a paper predicting that rockets would one day take people to the Moon and beyond, the American scientist Robert Goddard was laughed at and called "Moon mad." Seven years later Goddard launched a rocket that climbed 185 feet (56 meters) at 60 miles (97 kilometers) per hour. Critics pointed out that Goddard's rocket had traveled only one seven-millionth of the way to the Moon, at only one four-hundredth the speed (24,300 miles, or 39,100 kilometers, per hour) a Moon-bound craft needs to escape Earth's gravity. Yet Goddard's 1926 flight is remembered as the start of modern rocketry.

More powerful rockets were built. They rose to heights of 50, 100, then 250 miles (80, 160, and 400 kilometers). A giant step in space travel was achieved on October 4, 1957, when the Soviet Union launched the first man-made satellite, *Sputnik I,* which orbited Earth at 18,000 miles (29,000 kilometers) per hour. In 1961 Alan Shepard became the first American to travel into space. After that, progress in space travel came fast and furious.

Robert Goddard (left) *launched his first liquid-fueled rocket in 1926. Russia used a three-stage rocket on October 4, 1957, to launch* Sputnik 1 (below), *the first artificial satellite.*

Until about the 1960s, many people still believed that Mars, Venus, and perhaps other planets were home to living creatures—although perhaps not "life as we know it." A handful of people still clung to the hope that there was primitive life on the Moon, despite its lack of air and water and temperatures ranging from −400°F to 250°F (−240°C to 121°C). But then astronauts landed on the Moon, and information-gathering devices called space probes reached every planet but Pluto. Generally speaking, the missions were great technological triumphs, but disappointing to those hoping to find extraterrestrials.

PROBING THE SOLAR SYSTEM

The Moon On July 20, 1969, *Apollo 11* astronauts Neil Armstrong and Edwin "Buzz" Aldrin became the first Earthlings to walk on another heavenly body when they stepped onto the Moon. As they gathered soil and rock samples and performed experiments, the astronauts saw for themselves that the Moon is a desolate world. However, scientists feared that the Moon might harbor some kind of unknown and deadly germs, so the astronauts were placed in isolation for 18 days upon their return to Earth. The quarantine ended only when it was proved that the astronauts and the samples they had brought back contained no Moon organisms.

Scientists isolated and tested a crushed Moon rock in a completely sterile laboratory.

Mercury The *Mariner 10* probe that zoomed past Mercury in 1974–75 showed that the innermost planet, with its craters and cliffs, resembles Earth's Moon. Inhospitable to life in every way, Mercury has 800°F (427°C) temperatures—hotter than an oven—and is dry and nearly airless.

Venus In 1990 the *Magellan* probe reached Venus, adding to the knowledge gained by earlier missions. No spacecraft has survived for even a few hours on Venus's nearly 900°F (482°C) surface, which is thought to contain puddles of glowing red metal. Moreover, the planet once known as "Earth's Twin" lacks water and oxygen, and its clouds contain gases that would poison humans.

Mars The *Viking 1* and *Viking 2* probes landed on the "Red Planet" in 1976 and obtained photographs and information that dampened the hopes of the believers in Martians. The lines that Giovanni Schiaparelli and Percival Lowell thought they saw on Mars were telescopic illusions rather than canals, and there are no cities on the Red Planet. Mars has –220°F (–140°C) temperatures and very little oxygen, and its water is frozen. Still, the book is not closed on Mars, as will be seen.

Jupiter The largest of the nine planets could hold 1,400 Earths, but stories of giant invaders from Jupiter must remain on the fiction shelves. The *Galileo* mission that reached Jupiter in 1995 learned that the planet is more like the Sun than scientists had expected. Jupiter seems to be all, or nearly all, gas and liquids. At its cloud tops Jupiter is a frigid –235°F (–148°C), but lower down it is a blazing 6,000°F (3,300°C). Huge lightning bolts flash through Jupiter's clouds, and 300-mile (500-kilometer)-per-hour winds shake the "Giant Planet."

Saturn In 1977 *Voyager 1* and *Voyager 2* were launched on a "Grand Tour" of Jupiter, Saturn, Uranus, and Neptune. When the twin probes approached Saturn in 1980–81, they found it to be similar to Jupiter in many ways. The poisonous gases of its atmosphere, as well as 1,000-mile (1,600-kilometer)-per-hour winds and –300°F (–185°C) temperatures, make the "Ringed Planet" a forbidding world.

Uranus *Voyager 2* passed near Uranus in 1986, revealing that it seems to be both too cold and too hot to support life. Uranus's clouds are colder than –300°F

(–185°C). Beneath them, Uranus seems to have an ocean, but we don't expect to find anyone fishing in it, for its temperature is in the thousands of degrees.

Neptune   Because of its color from up close, Neptune has recently been nicknamed the "Blue Planet." But Neptune's handsome looks are deceiving. The Blue Planet's 600-mile (1,000-kilometer)-per-hour winds, –360°F (–218°C) temperature, and poisonous gas clouds make the surface of our Moon seem almost pleasant by contrast.

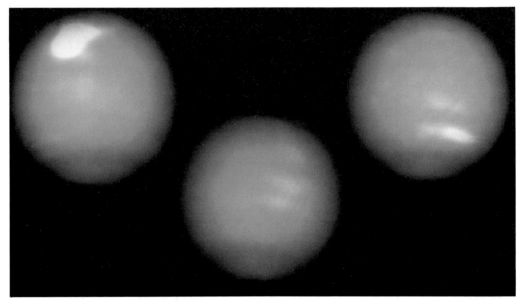

These images of Neptune were taken by the Hubble Space Telescope in 1994 when Neptune was 2.8 billion miles (4.5 billion kilometers) from Earth.

Pluto   In 1930 Clyde Tombaugh of Lowell Observatory discovered our solar system's ninth planet. Hundreds of suggestions for names for the planet poured into the observatory. The staff voted and chose the name Pluto, for the Roman god of the dead, which eleven-year-old Venetia Burney of Oxford, England, had proposed. The name is fitting. No space probe has gone there, but observations from afar indicate that Pluto is a frigid –400°F (–240°C). Clyde Tombaugh has called the planet he discovered a "huge iceberg"; however, its ice seems to contain frozen poisonous gases.

Planet X Most astronomers think that all of the Sun's planets have been discovered. However, some believe that Uranus and Neptune don't follow the orbits they should according to Newton's laws of gravitation and that a tenth planet is pulling them out of position. In mathematics and science, X means the unknown, so the theoretical planet is referred to as Planet X. Several scientists are currently trying to calculate Planet X's position so that telescopes can be aimed at the proper location to find it. They include University of Maryland astronomer Dr. Tom Van Flandern and rocket scientist Dr. Conley Powell of Teledyne Brown Engineering in Huntsville, Alabama. If the tenth planet exists, it is very distant from the Sun and must be incredibly cold and lifeless.

One planet has been omitted from our tour of the solar system. Like the baby bear's porridge, the third planet from the Sun is "just right" for life. Its average temperature is a comfortable 57°F (14°C), and it has plenty of water, which every plant and animal we know of requires. The planet's atmosphere, roughly 80 percent nitrogen and 20 percent oxygen, is also ideal for life. Of course this planet is our own beautiful Earth!

OTHER MOONS

Most astronomers today are convinced that Earth is the only place in the solar system that is home to intelligent life. Yet they are hopeful that simpler forms of life may exist on other bodies in the solar system.

Several moons that orbit planets may have the potential to support life. Titan, the largest of Saturn's more than 20 moons, is about the same size as the planet Mercury. Titan has a thick atmosphere composed primarily of nitrogen. Scientists find this intriguing, because Earth's atmosphere is also composed mostly of nitrogen. In a cooperative venture, the U.S. space agency (NASA) and the European Space Agency are planning to send a spacecraft to explore Saturn and Titan. Called *Cassini,* it is scheduled for launch in 1997 with an arrival date at the Ringed Planet seven years later, in 2004. *Cassini* will be programmed to release a probe that will descend to Titan's surface by parachute. The probe is expected to gather data that will help scientists determine many facts about Titan, including whether it is home to primitive forms of life.

The *Galileo* craft that began orbiting Jupiter in 1995 has made some exciting discoveries about Europa, one of the largest of the Giant Planet's 16 known moons. Europa may have an atmosphere and temperatures that are warm enough to support life. Moreover, Europa may have underground oceans beneath its cracked landscape. In the late 1990s the *Galileo* craft will make further observations of Europa to help determine whether simple organisms might live there.

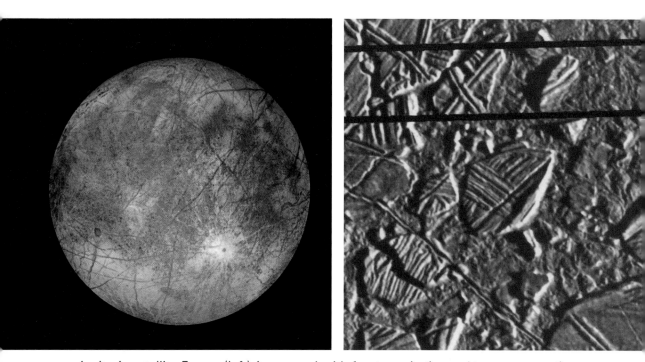

Jupiter's satellite Europa (left) *is covered with fractures in the crust, some more than 1,850 miles (3,000 kilometers) long. The high-resolution photo* (right) *was taken from the* Galileo *spacecraft on February 20, 1997, during a close fly-by. It clearly shows ice crustal plates. These resemble the pack-ice during spring thaws on Earth.*

THE MYSTERIES OF MARS

The most exciting prospect concerns Mars. Although the Red Planet seems to be hostile to life today, apparently this was not always so. Photographs taken by probes sent there during the 1970s show that Mars has dry riverbeds. "This indicates that Mars once had liquid water, which is necessary for life," explains planetary scientist Dr. John Stansberry of Lowell Observatory. He adds that in the past, Mars may have been considerably warmer than it is today. "Also," he continues, "Mars seems to have lost a lot of its atmosphere over billions of years, so it may have once had more of the gases that life as we know it needs. Possibly Mars was home to plants and animals back when it had water and a richer atmosphere."

Recently scientists have found clues that at least primitive life may have once existed on Mars. Among other things, the *Viking* probes tested the Red Planet's atmosphere and soil. From these tests, it was learned that Mars rocks have a chemical composition that distinguishes them from Earth rocks. About 12 rocks believed to have come from Mars have been discovered on Earth. Scientists speculate that large objects such as asteroids slammed into Mars long ago and hurled the rocks into space, where they floated about until swept in by Earth's gravity.

In the summer of 1996, a team of scientists from NASA and several universities announced that a 4½-pound (2-kilogram) rock found near Earth's South Pole seems to have come from Mars, and that microscopic shapes in the rock resemble bacteria on Earth. The scientists believe that these shapes are microfossils—the remains of microscopic organisms that lived on Mars several billion years ago.

If further studies prove beyond a doubt that the rock contains Martian microfossils, it will be one of the greatest scientific breakthroughs in history. Not only would we have the first evidence of extraterrestrial organisms, the discovery would imply that life is not rare but tends to occur naturally on planets with proper conditions. Furthermore, our hopes would be raised that Mars was once home to plants and animals, and that perhaps primitive organisms exist there today.

The United States plans to determine whether Mars has or has ever had life.

ALH84001,0

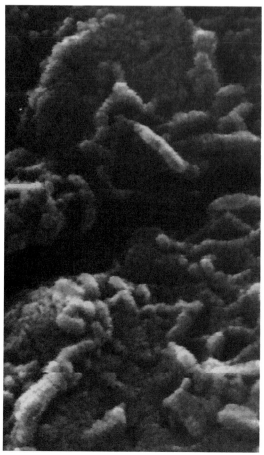

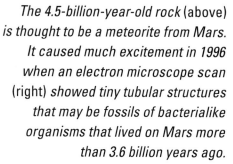

The 4.5-billion-year-old rock (above) *is thought to be a meteorite from Mars. It caused much excitement in 1996 when an electron microscope scan* (right) *showed tiny tubular structures that may be fossils of bacterialike organisms that lived on Mars more than 3.6 billion years ago.*

Douglas Isbell, NASA public affairs officer, says that the U.S. space program will focus much of its attention on exploring Mars at the end of the twentieth and the beginning of the twenty-first centuries. The *Mars Global Survey* is a probe that will eventually map the entire planet from orbit. As an exciting first step in the exploration of Mars, NASA successfully landed a probe, *Mars Pathfinder*, on July 4, 1997. *Pathfinder* traveled over 119 million miles to reach Mars. It slowed from its speed through space of 17,000 mph to a mere 60 mph before touching down on rocky terrain. When its "petals" unfolded, solar cells provided power to transmit the first pictures of the Mars surface to Earth. Later, a robot rover about

The rover is part of the Mars Pathfinder *probe. It is capable of analyzing the composition of surface rock.*

the size of a microwave oven was released to explore the surface of Mars and to analyze air and soil samples. Scientists will study this data for years to come.

NASA has even grander plans a few years down the road. "Around 2005 we will probably send a Mars Sample Return Mission to bring pieces of Mars back to Earth so that we can analyze them for primitive life," says Isbell. "But it will probably take human beings to actually search for plant and animal fossils," he says. "Missions to Mars during which astronauts land and do the fossil searches might come sometime around 2018."

Because astronauts are generally in their thirties when they embark on major missions, perhaps someone reading this book will do what humans have dreamed about for centuries—land on Mars and search for signs of life.

3

Solar Systems Beyond

Astronomers have figured that there are a hundred stars for every grain of sand on all of Earth's beaches. It's impossible that all those stars are lifeless. There must be trillions if not quadrillions of planets out there with aliens on them—even if only one star in a million has a planet with life.

—CLYDE TOMBAUGH, DISCOVERER OF PLUTO

It would be tremendously exciting to discover that plants and animals once inhabited Mars, or that primitive organisms can be found on Europa and Titan. Yet despite the fact that we would be happy to find any kind of life, we are most interested in *intelligent* life—creatures with the thinking ability to understand mathematics and build telescopes and spacecraft. Earth seems to be the only place in the solar system that has ever had intelligent life, yet that doesn't mean the quest to find extraterrestrial intelligence is doomed. The solar system is very important to us, but it is only a small part of an incredibly big universe.

COUNTING STARS

On certain nights in a dark place, what looks like a whitish band of light can be seen stretching across the heavens. Long ago it was named the Milky Way for its appearance, but a telescope reveals that, as Galileo learned four centuries ago, it is composed of stars so numerous they look like a stream of milk to the naked eye. The Milky Way is a *galaxy*—a gigantic island of stars moving together through space. Galileo was right when he said that the number of stars in the Milky Way is "almost beyond belief." According to recent thinking, our Sun is one of an estimated trillion (1,000,000,000,000) stars in the Milky Way galaxy. At a rate of one star per second, it would take 30,000 years to count every star in our galaxy.

Just as the Sun is a small part of the Milky Way, that huge island of stars is merely one among billions of galaxies. In January 1996 astronomers announced that new data from the Hubble Space Telescope indicates that the universe contains more than 50 billion galaxies—five times as many as previously thought. Since the Milky Way is a rather typical galaxy, we can figure that galaxies average about a trillion stars each. This means that the entire universe contains more than 50 sextillion (50,000,000,000,000,000,000,000) stars. At a rate of a billion stars per second, a computer would need more than a million years to count every star in the universe.

The fact that there are five times as many galaxies as had been believed is wonderful news for people who hope to discover extraterrestrials. Judging by our solar system, we know that stars can be accompanied by planets. So, more stars means more chances for planets—and more possibilities for intelligent life.

Most astronomers have long been convinced that due to the sheer number of stars, many of them must have planets with thinking creatures. Their reasoning had two problems. First, what if planet formation is highly unusual or even unique to the Sun? Second, what if the process of creating intelligent life is so complex that the odds are against its occurring anywhere else? Let's consider these problems one at a time.

OTHER STARS HAVE PLANETS!

An obstacle to determining whether planets orbit other stars is that they would be too dim to show up in our existing optical telescopes. Nevertheless, astronomers found evidence in the 1990s that planets seem to be common.

Heavenly bodies don't just produce the light we see—they also emit waves our eyes can't see, including radio waves. Astronomers study the natural radio emissions of heavenly bodies with dish-shaped instruments called radio telescopes. One important discovery made with radio telescopes came in the 1960s, when astronomers located pulsars, fast-spinning stars that emit detectable radio pulses each time they rotate. Pulsars spin with astonishing speed—typically twice per second. One variety, millisecond pulsars, rotate even faster. A millisecond is a thousandth of a second, and a millisecond pulsar completes one spin in several thousandths of a second. Millisecond pulsars send out radio pulses at such reliably regular intervals that they keep time similarly to the most accurate clocks ever devised by humans—atomic clocks.

In 1990 Cornell University radio astronomer Alex Wolszczan was searching for millisecond pulsars with one of the world's great radio telescopes, the 1,000-foot (300-meter) dish at Puerto Rico's Arecibo Observatory. That February he discovered a millisecond pulsar about 1,500 light-years from the Sun. The Polish-born radio astronomer found that this star, named PSR 1257+12, sent out a pulse once every 6.2 milliseconds, which meant that it was spinning 161 times per second. But there was something extremely peculiar about PSR 1257+12. Sometimes its pulses arrived a little earlier than they were supposed to, and at other times a bit late. This was equivalent to an atomic clock that ran a little fast and then a little slow for no apparent reason. "Millisecond pulsars don't behave this way!" Dr. Wolszczan told himself when he discovered this oddity.

As he monitored PSR 1257+12, Wolszczan learned that its pulse rate varied in regular patterns. One cycle required 66.2 days, and another 98.2 days, to complete. Why did this distant star's pulse rate change in regular cycles? Back at Cornell University, in Ithaca, New York, he plugged his data into his computer and analyzed it. "By the summer of 1991 I was excited because I was starting to suspect what might be the cause," Wolszczan remembers.

Because the Sun is so much larger than the planets (it could contain about 1,000 Jupiters) and its gravitation holds the planets in orbit, a fact is often overlooked. The planets also have a tiny influence on the Sun. Due to the planets' gravitational pull, the Sun wobbles slightly as the solar system travels through the Milky Way.

In the fall of 1991, Wolszczan reached a startling conclusion. The only possi-

This 60-foot (18-meter) radio telescope is similar to the radio telescopes in use in 1960 when pulsars were first detected.

ble explanation for the pulse variations was that the gravitation of at least two planets was causing PSR 1257+12 to wobble, sometimes toward us and sometimes farther away. When the pulsar wobbled away from us, its pulses arrived a bit behind schedule. When it wobbled toward us, they arrived slightly early. Wolszczan concluded that the 66.2- and 98.2-day cycles were caused by planets that take 66.2 and 98.2 days, respectively, to orbit the star. Since then, Wolszczan has determined that a third and perhaps a fourth planet also orbit the pulsar. Other scientists agreed with Dr. Wolszczan's conclusions and hailed him as the first discoverer of extrasolar planets (planets orbiting stars other than our Sun).

Life couldn't exist on PSR 1257+12's planets, because pulsars emit deadly X rays. Yet the discovery is a clue that intelligent life is probably common elsewhere in the universe. Pulsars, which are the cores of exploded stars, are one of the last places astronomers had expected to find planets. If a pulsar has planets, it seems likely that many normal stars do, too, and that some of them must have conditions that are friendly to life.

Over the past few years, several astronomers have tried to detect planets orbiting Sunlike stars—a type that they know can have a planet with intelligent life. Their main technique has been to attach spectrographs to optical telescopes. Spectrographs make detailed records of the various colors in the light from a star, which is called its spectrum. By analyzing star spectrums, astronomers can determine their temperatures, chemical composition, and direction of movement. The extrasolar planet hunters searched for Sunlike stars that wobbled a little as they traveled through space, which could mean that they had large planets tugging them slightly out of position.

In the spring of 1994 Michel Mayor and Didier Queloz of Switzerland's Geneva Observatory began studying 150 Sunlike stars spectrographically, in search of wobbles caused by planets. On October 6, 1995, they announced that they had discovered a massive planet pulling at 51 Pegasi (called 51 Peg for short), a star 50 light-years away in the constellation Pegasus the Winged Horse. This was a landmark discovery, for it was the first extrasolar planet found around a Sunlike star.

Meanwhile, Geoffrey Marcy and Paul Butler were running a spectrographic planet hunt at California's Lick Observatory. In 1996 they announced that they

An artist's rendition of how a spectrometer (the prisms) spreads starlight (the rays from the flat disks) into its composite colors (the color bands). Astronomers analyze the colors to detect planets around other stars.

had found huge planets orbiting three Sunlike stars: 47 Ursae Majoris (in the constellation the Great Bear, also called the Big Dipper), 70 Virginis (in Virgo the Virgin), and 55 Cancri (in Cancer the Crab). Also in 1996 several astronomers, including William Cochran of the University of Texas, announced their discovery of another extrasolar planet. Nearly twice the size of Jupiter, this planet orbits 16 Cygni (a star in the constellation Cygnus the Swan, commonly called the Northern Cross). By 1997, astronomers had discovered at least twelve planets orbiting Sunlike stars.

Locating a few planets by indirect means has convinced astronomers that planets are plentiful. At the present, however, they can only detect huge planets without being able to see them. In the future, they hope to develop the ability to not only detect smaller, Earthlike worlds but to actually view them.

NASA is planning to build a planetary-search telescope that could accomplish this. Called the Planet Finder, it may be launched into an orbit 500 million miles (800 million kilometers) from the Sun. From that location—roughly the distance of Jupiter—the Planet Finder would be beyond the atmosphere and dust that obstruct our view of the stars from on and near Earth. Construction of the telescope, which could cost $3 billion, is likely to be under way by the year 2015. The results should be worth the time and money. With the Planet Finder, explains NASA Public Affairs Officer Don Savage, "Astronomers should be able to tell whether a planet has water and an atmosphere that could support life." The instrument may even enable astronomers to study continents and oceans on Earthlike planets.

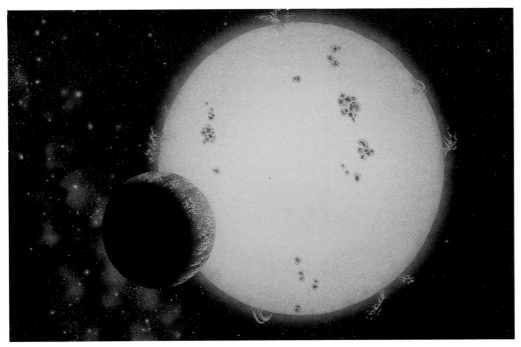

In this painting, an artist shows how the first extrasolar planet found around a Sunlike star, 51 Pegasi, might look. The planet was detected by means of spectrographs in October 1995.

A UNIQUE ACCIDENT?

Although planets may be commonplace, there is still the second problem with assuming that intelligent life must exist on some of them: What if the processes involved in the creation of intelligent life are so complex that they wouldn't be likely to occur more than once? We cannot answer this question with certainty, but there are indications that we probably have plenty of company in the universe.

During the 1950s, chemists Harold Urey and Stanley Miller conducted a famous experiment. They mixed substances that should be plentiful on many planets—water, hydrogen, ammonia, and methane—in a bottle. They gave their chemical stew electric shocks to simulate lightning, which may have helped spark the creation of simple life on Earth. After a week, amino acids had formed. This was an exciting development, because amino acids are the building blocks of proteins, and proteins are basic to life. The results indicated that at least simple life should be common throughout the cosmos.

Discoveries made in the past few years point to the same conclusion. For one thing, life has been found to be more durable than had been thought. Simple organisms have been found deep inside the frozen ground in Siberia, and even inside rocks in Antarctica. Also, life appeared earlier than scientists once believed. "Life began on Earth when the water in the oceans stopped boiling, as if it were waiting to happen," says Dr. Mike Davis of Arecibo Observatory. "This means that life almost certainly exists on lots of other planets. The big question is, has advanced life—creatures like dinosaurs and human beings—developed on some of those planets? We do not completely understand how advanced life came about and some people still argue that it was a unique accident that occurred only on Earth."

Most scientists see no reason to believe that intelligent life is a unique accident. Rocket scientist Dr. Conley Powell expresses the prevailing view when he says, "I would be astonished if we *didn't* eventually find intelligent life elsewhere in the universe." Astronomer Mark Littmann of the University of Tennessee at Knoxville agrees. "Since planet formation seems to be common, the possibility of life on other planets is much greater than what we had earlier believed," says Dr. Littmann. "I think intelligent life on other planets has to exist in wild abundance."

The discoverer of Pluto also believed that extraterrestrials must be plentiful. "It's probably normal for stars to have planets," Clyde Tombaugh explained shortly before his death in early 1997. "Some must be at the right distance and have the right chemical conditions to support life. As we speak, there must be trillions of planets out there with alien civilizations on them." The 90-year-old astronomer had a pet peeve on the subject. "It burns me up when they have these Miss Universe contests and call the winner the most beautiful girl in the universe," said Tombaugh. "How do we know what kind of beauty pageants they have on other planets?" Of course, beauty is definitely in the eye of the beholder in this case, for the winners on other planets may have three heads or look like spiders.

Ideas and opinions can take us only so far on the issue of extraterrestrial intelligence, however. Astronomy has many examples of ideas that made sense at the time but later proved to be false. What science requires is proof. The fact is, there are only three ways to prove the existence of extraterrestrials: We can visit other planets and find them; they can visit us here on Earth; or we can exchange signals with each other.

4

Off to
the Stars!

One day we should be able to build spaceships that can travel half of, or even close to, the speed of light. All it takes is money and the will to do it.

—Charles Kowal, Operations Astronomer, Space Telescope Science Institute

Star Trek's immense popularity shows that the idea of visiting the inhabitants of other planetary systems intrigues people. But doing so in reality is not as easy as it appears in the TV shows and movies in which space explorers press a button and make interstellar journeys (voyages between the stars) in a few minutes. Escaping the Sun's gravity is not the main problem, for we have already sent several space probes beyond the solar system. They include the twin *Voyagers*, which by 1997 were heading out into interstellar space. Because of the remote possibility that a distant civilization will find the *Voyagers* ages from now, they have been equipped with messages from Earth, including images of children and animals and recordings of laughter and music.

WAY OUT THERE

The main barrier to visiting other planetary systems is the length of the voyages. So vast are interstellar distances that astronomers measure them not in miles but in light-years. A light-year is the distance that light, which moves at 186,282 miles (300,000 kilometers) per second, travels in a year. For people who think in miles, a light-year equals 5,880,000,000,000 (5.88 trillion) miles, or 9,500,000,000,000 (9.5 trillion) kilometers.

Proxima Centauri, the star closest to the Sun, is 4.3 light-years, or 25 trillion miles (40 trillion kilometers), away. At the rate *Voyager 1* and *2* are traveling—about 35,000 miles (56,000 kilometers) per hour—they would reach Proxima Centauri in approximately 80,000 years—were they aimed in its direction. More distant destinations would require more time. Even at a speed of a million miles (1.6 million kilometers) per hour, a trip to the Andromeda galaxy, 2.2 million light-years away, would take 1.5 *billion* years.

Voyager 1 was launched into space in 1977 along with Voyager 2. In approximately 285,000 years, Voyager 2 will approach within 3.5 light-years of Sirius, the brightest star in our night sky.

Because of the length of the voyages, for many years there was little interest in interstellar travel except in science-fiction stories, films, and TV shows. Why try to build a starship when we didn't know if there were any planets beyond the solar system to visit? Recent developments have changed the picture completely, says rocket scientist Dr. Conley Powell. "Unquestionably there is more interest in interstellar travel of late because of the discovery of extrasolar planets," explains Powell. "Now we can be reasonably certain that there will be something to explore at the end of an interstellar voyage."

There may be nearly as many ideas about how to make interstellar journeys as there are people interested in the topic. Many scientists favor sending robots that would explore distant planetary systems and transmit the data back to Earth. Made of metal and plastic, the robots won't care if a trip takes a thousand years or a million years. Launching robots to extrasolar planets is a possibility, since we have already built robot devices to conduct experiments on Mars and Venus.

"However," says Conley Powell, "we are impatient critters and might find it difficult to wait many years for the results of a probe mission before sending out human beings. I believe that if we build the Planet Finder and detect Earthlike planets, we might skip probes entirely and send off human explorers without waiting for any more information." Dr. Powell explains that there are several ways for human beings to make voyages that might last thousands of years.

DEEP-FREEZE TRAVEL

One idea is sometimes called the "Rip Van Winkle" plan. Named for the character in the Washington Irving story who falls asleep for 20 years, this technique would place astronauts in a frozen sleep so that they wouldn't age during space voyages lasting centuries. A big problem with this plan is that under ordinary conditions ice expands, forming crystals that would destroy the body's cells. But if a protective substance for the cells is ever developed (sometimes called a "human antifreeze"), we may be able to send astronauts through space like packages of frozen peas, and then thaw and awaken them at journey's end.

There may even be a way to pursue the "Rip Van Winkle" technique without a "human antifreeze," adds Dr. Powell. At a sufficiently high pressure, water does not expand when it freezes, he explains. So, if we learned to freeze the astronauts at a high pressure and then safely thaw them, we could avoid the deadly expansion of ice crystals in their bodies.

A SPEEDING COLONY

Another way to send people off on a long space voyage is to create an "interstellar space colony"—an enormous craft in which families would live for many generations while traveling to another planetary system. This idea has been extensively investigated by the Space Studies Institute, a Princeton, New Jersey, organization that researches methods for utilizing the resources of space.

Bettie Greber, the Institute's executive director, explains that the colony might be assembled at a point in space about a quarter of a million miles (400,000 kilometers) from Earth. The Moon could provide most of the materials for creating the colony, including such building supplies as silicon (for glass and fiberglass), iron, and aluminum. Oxygen, which the space colonists would need to breathe, could be extracted from the Moon's soil. Because the Moon has much less gravity than the Earth, an electric motor called a mass driver could launch materials from there to the space colony building site without much difficulty.

A few of the original materials for the colony would come from Earth. These might include hydrogen, which when combined with oxygen from Moon soil would produce H_2O—water. But once on its interstellar journey, the colony would be self-sufficient. For example, it would purify and reuse its water endlessly, so that no more would ever be needed after the initial supply.

"The space colony will be very large—several miles in diameter," predicts Greber. "Many people think a huge ball with smaller balls on either end is the best shape, but a space colony might also be shaped like a giant bicycle wheel or perhaps a cylinder." The travelers won't feel that they are in a moving craft far from home because the colony will spin to provide it with an Earthlike gravity. On a spherical colony, for example, the people would live on the inner curve of the ball.

The colony will resemble a small town, Greber explains. The only difference

Building a space colony would require international cooperation. In 1995 American astronauts and Russian cosmonauts began to routinely fly on each other's spacecraft. Astronaut Shannon Lucid (left) is shown here with two Russian cosmonauts on board Russia's Mir *space station. When Lucid returned to Earth on September 26, 1996, she had spent 188 consecutive days in space—a record for the longest space flight by a woman and by an American.*

will be that no one could move away. Century after century, the travelers will be born, marry, have children and grandchildren, and die on the colony until the huge craft reaches its destination. Because garbage and other wastes will be recycled, and dead bodies will be cremated and sprinkled in the space colony soil, no debris from the huge starship will be ejected into space.

"About ten thousand people will live in the space colony," Greber believes. "It will have streets, sidewalks, homes, houses of worship, parks, trees, schools, lakes, and maybe even a small river. People will have the same jobs we have on Earth." The colony's farmers will produce food for the voyagers by raising live-stock and growing crops in a smaller sphere outside the main living quarters. Plants produce oxygen, so by growing them the colonists will not only produce food; they will also replenish their oxygen supply. A second sphere outside the living quarters will be used for manufacturing and scientific research. "Perhaps the space colony scientists will invent faster propulsion systems so that while the colony is already in motion they will find ways to increase its speed," says Greber.

The first space colonies will be located in the solar system. "If we began work on it now, we could have a full-sized space colony operating in our solar system in twenty years," predicts Bettie Greber. She concludes: "I think by the end of the twenty-first century we could build a space colony that could keep moving through space for thousands of years to explore another planetary system."

A COSMIC SPEED LIMIT

Perhaps we will design robots that will explore far-off worlds. We may find as-tronauts willing to be frozen for a few million years, or people ready to put down all the roots of their family tree in a space colony. Still, the time problem remains, for even if we could achieve a speed of a million miles (1.6 million kilo-meters) per hour, a round-trip flight to the Andromeda galaxy would require 3 billion years. By the time the robots, frozen astronauts, or space families re-turned to Earth, we may have forgotten about the expedition, moved away from our dying planet, or disappeared like the dinosaurs.

As of 1997, the speed record for people in space was 25,000 miles (40,000 kilometers) per hour—400 times as fast as Robert Goddard's pioneering rocket flight. Perhaps in the twenty-first century we will build starships that can move 400 times as fast as today's spacecraft, or 10 million miles (16 million kilometers) per hour. And in the century after that we may build space vehicles capable of still faster speeds.

This Russian-built rover "Marsokhod" is designed to explore the surface of Mars in 1998.

However, there is a limit to how fast we can ultimately travel. According to physicist Albert Einstein's special theory of relativity, a spacecraft's maximum speed is just under the speed of light. We needn't feel that nature has played a cruel trick on us by setting this cosmic speed limit, for it is incredibly fast. Traveling at nearly 186,282 miles (300,000 kilometers) per second, we could go from the Earth to the Moon in just over a second!

A tremendous roadblock stands in the way of our achieving the cosmic speed limit. If our starship carried its fuel along, as spacecraft do now, and used a fuel similar to what is available today, it would require a gigantic supply to approach the speed of light. One scientist calculated that 1,000,000,000,000,000,000,000,000,000,000,000,000,000,000 (1 tredecillion) pounds (0.45 tredecillion kilograms) of rocket fuel would be needed—more than the Earth weighs. As a result, many scientists, including physicist Daniel P. Whitmire of the University of Louisiana at Lafayette and Clyde Tombaugh, have concluded that we will never come close to approaching the speed of light.

Dr. Whitmire points out that physics (the study of matter and energy and how they interact) says that approaching the speed of light *is* possible. But, he adds, there is a difference between what is possible in theory and what can actually be achieved. Whitmire thinks that we will probably never overcome the fuel-weight problem. He says, "Even using nuclear fuel would require huge amounts of energy, and even then we would only be able to get up to a small percentage of the speed of light. I don't think human beings will ever make interstellar flights." Said Tombaugh: "It will always be impractical for us to go to other stars. It would take many millions of tons of fuel to travel at just one percent of the speed of light to the nearest star, meaning a 430-year trip to Proxima Centauri. Looking for an undiscovered way of getting there is out of the question, because there is no super-fuel."

Some rocket scientists and physicists think we may find super-fuels, and they have dreamed up designs for spacecraft much more powerful than today's. Most of the proposed starships may never be built, due to cost, construction difficulties, and the dangers of flying in the vehicles. Yet who knows? An idea or two might revolutionize future space travel.

SPACECRAFT OF THE FUTURE

One plan is to propel a spacecraft by exploding nuclear bombs out its rear, which would offer the added bonus of helping rid the world of nuclear weapons. Dr. Mike Davis of Puerto Rico's Arecibo Observatory thinks that "probably the most efficient way of achieving great speeds is to use hydrogen bombs with a shield to block the blast from harming the ship." But this method probably could move a spaceship at "only" 2,000 miles (3,200 kilometers) per second—the 1 percent of the speed of light to which Clyde Tombaugh referred.

A craft called the fusion rocket could achieve much greater speeds than 2,000 miles per second, says Dr. Conley Powell. The fusion rocket would operate through the same principles by which stars and hydrogen bombs produce their enormous energy. Everything in the universe is made of tiny units called atoms. In a fusion rocket the nuclei (centers) of atoms would be fused, or joined together, under very hot conditions, producing a gaslike substance called plasma that would be shot out the back of the rocket, propelling it at tremendous speeds. "We could build a fusion rocket in the near future that could achieve speeds of 100 million miles [160 million kilometers] per hour, or fifteen percent of the speed of light," says Powell, who thinks that atoms of a form of hydrogen called deuterium and a type of helium called helium-3 could be used in the fusion reaction. "Fusion rockets could power the monstrously large ships that some people believe will be sent out as interstellar space colonies," he explains.

Another craft that would work by nuclear fusion might be more difficult to build but faster than the fusion rocket. Called the interstellar ramjet, it wouldn't need to take much fuel along. Instead, the vessel would "scoop up" most of its fuel as it traveled from star to star. The space between stars is not completely empty. Hydrogen atoms are scattered about. A magnetic scooper to gather hydrogen would be attached to the spacecraft. Through a fusion reaction similar to the way the Sun creates heat and light, the starship would convert the hydrogen into massive amounts of energy. The ship's route might even be planned to take it through "interstellar gas stations"—gas clouds in space where hydrogen is plentiful. An interstellar ramjet should be able to approach the speed of light, its backers claim.

Conley Powell thinks that a vehicle combining aspects of both the fusion rocket and the interstellar ramjet may one day be built. Called the ram-augmented interstellar rocket, this craft would scoop up hydrogen that would be added to the propulsion system of a fusion rocket. "The ram-augmented interstellar rocket could provide more thrust than either system would have alone," says Dr. Powell.

The ion-propulsion spaceship, also called the ion-gun engine, might also be capable of approaching the speed of light. Although atoms generally have no electric charge, they sometimes gain or lose electrons. They then become electrically charged and are known as ions. An ion-propulsion spaceship would employ a fuel that could easily be changed into ions, such as mercury, which is used in fluorescent lamps and some thermometers. An electric generator would ionize the fuel. Electric fields would attract the ionized atoms and shoot them like a gun out the rear of the rocket. "An ion-propulsion spaceship would accelerate slowly," says Charles Kowal, operations astronomer for the Hubble Space Telescope, which was launched into orbit above Earth in 1990. "But it could keep going faster and faster for a long time so that it might get close to the speed of light. If we had the money and the will to do it, we could build a small version of such a spacecraft right now."

One of the most unusual proposals involves antimatter. Each kind of particle that makes up atoms has a type of particle that is exactly the same but has an opposite electric charge. For example, electrons have a negative charge. Electrons have a kind of antimatter called a positron, which have a positive charge. In 1996 physicists working in Switzerland announced that they had created the first whole antimatter atoms—nine antihydrogen atoms. When antimatter and matter meet, they destroy each other, releasing a burst of energy. Scientists may eventually learn to create and store large amounts of antimatter. If placed in a starship and mixed with ordinary matter, the "big bangs" produced could propel the vessel at incredible speeds.

There are more ideas. Some say that sunlight and other starlight could help push a nuclear-powered craft at high velocities. Others talk of laser-powered interstellar vessels. Yet even if we actually build starships that can approach the speed of light, there still seems to be a difficulty in exploring the universe. Fewer than 1,000 stars lie within 40 light-years of Earth. Most stars are millions or billions of light-years away. Wouldn't a round-trip voyage to search for life on remote planets require millions or billions of years, even at the fastest speed possible?

The answer is yes and no.

TIME VARIES

Einstein's special theory of relativity explains that time does not always work in the way to which we are accustomed. Instead, time is relative to speed. A person traveling on a spaceship ages more slowly relative to a person on Earth. Called "time dilation," this effect has been proved in laboratories.

Time dilation increases greatly as a spacecraft approaches the speed of light. Imagine 30-year-old twins, one of whom is an astronaut and the other of whom remains on Earth. The astronaut embarks on what seems to him to be a 20-year voyage at a speed of 168,000 miles (270,000 kilometers) per second, or 90 percent of the speed of light. The astronaut returns to Earth 50 years old, only to find that his twin is 70 years old. The astronaut doesn't feel that he has cheated time. During his voyage, time seemed to pass at the same rate he was used to on Earth, and he marked off 20 years on his spaceship calendar. However, the 20 years at the high speed he was traveling was equal to 40 years of Earth time.

At a velocity of 99 percent of the speed of light, or 184,000 miles (295,000 kilometers) per second, time dilation becomes more extreme. Imagine that a 30-year-old astronaut leaves her 2-year-old son on Earth and goes on what seems to her to be a 12-year voyage at 99 percent of the speed of light. The astronaut returns to Earth in her early forties. But the young son she left behind is now about 90 years old—twice as old as his mother!

Traveling very, very near the speed of light, time would nearly grind to a halt for the space voyager in comparison to Earth time. In fact, it has been calculated that an astronaut traveling at a speed approaching 186,282 miles (300,000 kilometers) per second could make a round-trip to the edges of the known universe and back within about 80 years of spaceship time. However, because billions of years would have passed on Earth, the returning 101-year-old astronaut who departed at age 21 would not find anybody on his or her home planet. Scientists estimate that 5 billion years from now, the Sun will begin to die. Humans will either move to another planet or die along with our star.

Which brings us to the drawback of time dilation. For the space explorers, time-slowing is of great help, but what about those on Earth eager for news from the expedition? Dozens of generations of people on our planet could live and die while an expedition was exploring just the Milky Way, let alone distant galaxies. It appears that no matter what speed we achieve, we will have to learn to be extremely patient if we ever send astronauts to search for life beyond the nearest stars.

But for those who hope to contact extraterrestrials within their own lifetimes, there are possibilities.

5

Extraterrestrial Visitors?

You don't have to go into space to find aliens. They're here! Many people claim to have seen extraterrestrials. Generally scientists refuse to listen to these people, and that's wrong.

—WALTER H. ANDRUS, JR., INTERNATIONAL DIRECTOR, MUTUAL UFO NETWORK

Ancient people have recorded seeing airborne objects believed by some to be spacecraft from other worlds. Tens of thousands of strange flying objects have been reported in recent centuries. For example,

- in 1762 two astronomers in Basel, Switzerland, claimed that they observed a huge "spindle-shaped" craft in the sky.
- People in London, England, in 1847 described a "spherical craft" that rose straight up through the clouds.
- Urbain Leverrier, a French scientist who codiscovered Neptune, reported seeing what looked like a glowing, tube-shaped craft over Paris in 1864.
- In 1874 a cone-shaped craft was reported over Oaxaca, Mexico.
- Ships' crews spotted what looked like "revolving wheels" in the sky over the Persian Gulf in both 1879 and 1901.

- Thousands of people in at least 19 states reported seeing a cigar-shaped "flying machine" over the United States in 1896 and 1897—several years before the Wright brothers invented the airplane.

In 1947 the reports suddenly became more frequent. That June 24, Kenneth Arnold was flying his plane near Mount Rainier in Washington State when he noticed nine disk-shaped objects moving at what he figured to be nearly 2,000 miles (3,200 kilometers) per hour. Arnold said that the objects flew "like saucers"—dishes that hold cups. Newspaper writers changed the wording to "flying saucers." Ever since, flying saucers have been reported regularly from around the world. Certain periods have so many sightings that they are known as "flying saucer waves."

Flying saucers are one of the most misunderstood and controversial subjects in science. To start with, many people deny that they are a scientific topic at all and insist that most flying saucer witnesses have mistaken such objects as aircraft, balloons, and planets for alien spacecraft. The "believers" and "debunkers" tend to dislike and distrust each other to the point where several authors have maintained feuds for years.

Even the term *flying saucer* annoys many people, for it implies that an object is a spacecraft. Often what looks like flying saucers proves to be a flock of birds or meteors. Because of such mistakes, most people on both sides of the argument prefer the term *unidentified flying objects* (*UFOs* for short). This term makes no judgment as to what an object really is but merely notes that its nature is unknown.

THE CASE AGAINST · · ·

Few scientists believe that UFOs come from other planets. The reasons are simple and can be briefly stated. First, the UFOs' speeds aren't fast enough to take them through space. Witnesses often estimate their velocity at a few hundred miles per hour—the speed of a jet airplane. Sometimes UFOs are reported to be moving at a few thousand miles per hour, but that is still too slow for space travel.

Second, we have never found anything that has been left behind by extraterrestrials. No scrap of unearthly metal from a flying saucer, let alone an entire spacecraft, has ever been retrieved. No space suit or piece of clothing of known extraterrestrial origin has ever been discovered. And, despite the rumors that the U.S. government keeps the bodies of dead extraterrestrials in secret locations, there never has been any proof that anyone has actually seen an extraterrestrial—alive or dead.

We have thousands of photographs of UFOs in the sky, but the expression "a picture is worth a thousand words" does not seem to apply to them. Some of the objects look like hats, Frisbees, and assorted children's toys flying through the air. Others show phenomena that seem to be identifiable, such as unusual clouds, weather balloons, and man-made satellites. We don't have a single photograph of an object that is likely to be a genuine spaceship from another world. And in an age when millions of people own portable video cameras, or camcorders, no one has produced an authentic video of an extraterrestrial, despite all the individuals who claim to have had alien encounters.

On a cloudy Illinois afternoon in May 1974, David Dorn took this photo (left) of a UFO. On October 27, 1979, on the east coast of South Island, New Zealand, this cluster of lights was photographed.

Astronomer Mark Littmann summarizes the general opinion among scientists. "No one has ever produced any physical evidence that UFOs come from another world," asserts Dr. Littmann. "Our planes and spacecraft leave behind telltale signs, but these 'aliens' never leave anything behind. They never crash, either." Also, like most scientists, Littmann thinks the bulk of UFO reports are misidentifications of ordinary objects. "When I was director of Hansen Planetarium in Salt Lake City, Utah, we would get reports of flying saucers regularly. I would go outside and see that the UFO was really Venus or a bright star rising."

THE CASE FOR · · ·

The believers say that flying saucers move much faster in space than when near Earth, and ask why spacecraft built by a superior civilization should crash, when our own airplanes rarely do so. While admitting the lack of concrete proof, they also claim that there is plenty of indirect evidence for the existence of alien spacecraft. UFOs have been seen by dozens of people at a time, tracked on radar, and observed making moves impossible for any aircraft built by humans. Moreover, while some reports seem too bizarre to be believed, others are difficult to ignore, as the following cases demonstrate:

- At 2:24 on the morning of September 3, 1965, a trembling young man named Norman Muscarello burst into the Exeter, New Hampshire, police station. So shaken that he could barely speak, Norman claimed that minutes earlier a huge UFO with red lights around its rim had swooped down at him as he walked home from his girlfriend's house. Patrolman Eugene Bertrand persuaded Norman to show him the field where he had seen the UFO.

  The patrolman and youth reached the field at nearly 3:00 A.M. At first nothing happened, but then the neighborhood dogs began howling and a round object with red lights around its rim rose from behind two pine trees.

  Muscarello and Bertrand ran back to the police car, from where the patrolman radioed headquarters. "I see the thing myself!" screamed Bertrand. For a few minutes they watched the UFO perform moves over the field that no airplane or helicopter could do. Meanwhile, Patrolman David Hunt, who had heard Bertrand's radio call, pulled up and also saw the mysterious object. The incident remains unexplained to this day.

• At 8:30 P.M. on January 12, 1990, Steven Kellermeyer was driving through the outskirts of Indianapolis, Indiana, with his daughters Grace, 9, Rachel, 11, and Sarah, 15. Suddenly Rachel asked, "What's that, Dad?" Through the car window, the Kellermeyers saw a round object with pulsating lights.

The 33-year-old accountant pulled the car into a driveway next to an old barn and opened the windows. For the next few minutes he and his daughters observed the object, which they figured to be a mile (1.6 kilometers) away and 500 feet (150 meters) above the ground. The lights around the edge of the UFO blinked on and off in a circular pattern—alternately red, white, green, and blue. Although it mostly hovered, the object sometimes tilted back and forth like a spinning top, convincing the Kellermeyers that it couldn't be a helicopter or blimp. During one tilt, a spotlight came on from beneath the UFO and seemed to search the ground. During another tilt, the Kellermeyers saw what appeared to be a dome atop the UFO.

"As we watched, we were awestruck and speechless," Steven Kellermeyer recalls. They pulled out of the driveway after several minutes, but the UFO seemed to follow them for a short time. "The girls were truly frightened that the UFO was chasing us," says Kellermeyer. "My youngest daughter had nightmares about the incident for years. To this day, we get chills when we talk about it among ourselves. We know what we saw, and we believe it was not of this world."

• People who have seen UFOs often do not want their real names used, for fear of ridicule. This is the case with a retired forest ranger we'll call Ed. On August 31, 1994, Ed was one of six retired men sitting around a campfire at an Indiana campground. At about 8:30 in the evening, Ed spotted a bright, glowing light through the trees. For a second he thought he was seeing the Moon, but when it moved, Ed and his friends observed that it was saucer-shaped and had a dome clearly visible at the top. The UFO passed out of view after about a minute, but in that time one of Ed's companions grabbed his camera and took several photographs of the object.

Several blimps were in the area that night, and some people think this object was one of them. Ed and the others disagree, because blimps don't have a dome at the top and can't move as fast as this object apparently did. Also, blimps make noise, but the mysterious airship was silent. "The object wasn't in any way like a blimp," Ed recalls. And what of the photographs? They show an object that looks like a flying saucer with a domed top. Then again, the object looks a little like a blimp. As Ed says, "It is still a UFO."

- Thousands of people saw strange lights in the Arizona night sky on March 13, 1997. A retired police officer in Paulden, Arizona, was the first to report the sighting. Soon phone lines to UFO reporting centers and to local police departments were jammed with reports of sightings. Witnesses generally agreed the lights were part of a huge, V-shaped, soundless object that moved slowly over Phoenix. Some people videotaped the event, which lasted 106 minutes. Many are convinced they saw an alien spaceship.

This is an enlargement of a photograph taken August 31, 1994, by Dennis Bickle, a pilot, while on a camping trip in Indiana. Other people in the area reported seeing an unidentified object similar to the one in the upper left corner of this photo.

CONTACT REAL OR IMAGINED?

Sometimes people claim to encounter humanoids (meaning "humanlike creatures") or other aliens on or near a UFO. One such story that came out of Russia in 1989 at first seems too bizarre to take seriously. According to reports, numerous residents of Voronezh, a city of nearly a million people, saw UFOs in the sky over a period of weeks. The witnesses included a former pilot, an economist, and an engineering student. Several times the UFOs landed, with the strangest event occurring on September 27.

At 6:30 that evening a group of children were playing soccer in a park when they spotted a reddish sphere. It hovered above the park, attracting a crowd of about 40 adults, who joined the soccer players. Finally, the UFO landed and out stepped a 10-foot-tall (3 meters) humanoid with what appeared to be a robot. A soccer player screamed in terror, and the alien supposedly froze him like a statue for a few minutes just by staring at him. The alien supposedly made another boy completely disappear for a short time. Only when the alien and the robot reentered the UFO and flew away did the teenager reappear.

This case could easily be dismissed as fake except for the large number of people involved. At least five Russian newspapers reported the events along with eyewitness accounts, and many of the young people drew pictures of the alleged flying sphere and its occupants.

The strangest and most puzzling UFO cases are those in which people claim to have been abducted or temporarily kidnapped by extraterrestrials. Although the first known report of what some would call a "UFO abduction" occurred in the 1890s, the phenomenon did not capture great popular attention until the famous Barney and Betty Hill case of 1961. That September the Hills were driving in New Hampshire when they noticed a UFO near their car. According to the couple, they were taken aboard the UFO, physically examined by humanoids who were curious about Earthlings, and released unharmed.

Since the Hills' experience, numerous people have claimed to have had similar encounters. In fact, so many people say they have been taken aboard UFOs by aliens that a conference on the subject was held at the Massachusetts Institute of Technology (MIT) in June of 1992. The "Abduction Study Conference" featured a dozen "abductees" as well as more than 50 medical doctors, physicists, psychologists, social workers, and others who have studied the phenomenon. The mere fact that the conference took place was a breakthrough in "UFOlogy," as the study of UFOs is called, because a few years ago it would have been impossible to attract dozens of prominent scientists to a conference on so weird a subject.

The conference revealed a great deal about the "UFO abductees." First, there are more of them than is generally realized. It is estimated that, in the United States alone, more than 100,000 people claim to have been abducted by aliens. Second, instead of seeking attention, they often are shy people who hate publicity. Third, their experiences tend to be similar from case to case. Typically they claim to have been taken aboard UFOs where they are examined by gray, 4-foot- (1.2-meter) tall humanoids. The aliens are often described as having huge foreheads, large eyes, and an ability to communicate with the victims through their minds.

Perhaps *victims* and *abductees* are not the proper words, says Andrea Pritchard, editor of *Alien Discussions*, a 1994 book on the conference proceedings. "People who can get through the initial fears generated by these experiences often find their lives changed for the better," Pritchard believes. "They have a broader view of what's important in life. Some feel a love for these alien beings. Some feel an interconnection between all living things and our Earth, and become more interested in helping other humans and in caring for our planet."

So what can we conclude about the people who claim to have been abducted by aliens? As with UFOs in general, there are sharp differences of opinion. The so-called "abductees" are liars or cannot separate dreams from reality, say the "debunkers." The fact that thousands of people claim to have had similar abduction experiences means that their stories are true, insist the "believers." There are also many people who have what may be the most scientific attitude about the subject: they admit that they just don't know.

THE SEARCH FOR ANSWERS CONTINUES

The late J. Allen Hynek, a Northwestern University astronomy professor, was the most prominent scientist to devote much of his life to studying UFOs. While investigating UFOs for the U.S. Air Force for many years, Dr. Hynek went from scoffing at what he called "the craze for flying saucers" to believing that UFOs deserve serious study. In 1973 he obeyed one of his favorite sayings—"A scientist should be curious and eager to find out"—and founded the Center for UFO Studies (CUFOS) to promote further study of the phenomenon. CUFOS, which is located in Chicago, and MUFON (the Mutual UFO Network), based in Seguin, Texas, are two of the leading organizations for studying UFOs. Both organizations take reports of sightings by telephone and letter, and interview people who have had UFO experiences.

"UFOs are worth studying because they are extremely interesting as well as a scientific puzzle," says Mark Rodeghier, CUFOS's scientific director. "They may be a bizarre phenomenon we don't know about, or perhaps they are extraterrestrial spacecraft. Unless we keep studying them, we won't find out."

"You don't have to go out into space to find aliens," declares Walter H. Andrus, Jr., international director of MUFON, the world's largest UFO organization. "Many people claim to have seen extraterrestrials. Any scientist who takes the time to look at the data will be convinced that UFOs and extraterrestrials exist."

To make the data easier to study, MUFON is computerizing the 20,000 reports in its files, a project Andrus thinks will take until after the year 2000 to complete. When the project is finished, researchers may find clues—such as the places and times UFOs most frequently appear—that will provide a clearer picture of the phenomenon. MUFON also has 2,500 field investigators who take reports on UFOs in every state and most nations. Each of them hopes to one day find the piece of an alien spacecraft, the remains of an extraterrestrial, or other evidence that will prove that our Earth has been visited by beings from other planets.

6

Long-Distance Conversations With ETs

SETI attempts to answer the questions: Are we alone in the universe? Is intelligent life common? These are among the most basic questions human beings can ask.

—Physicist Dr. Daniel P. Whitmire

In the late 1930s radio engineer Grote Reber built a dish-shaped radio antenna in his Wheaton, Illinois, backyard. When Reber aimed his 31-foot-diameter (9.5 meters) dish at our Milky Way galaxy, he found that heavenly bodies emit natural radio signals. His instrument was the world's first radio telescope.

Since then, much larger and more powerful radio telescopes have been built. Radio telescopes have been called the "ears of astronomy," yet astronomers generally don't listen with them in the way that we listen to a radio. A radio telescope has at least one bowl-shaped dish antenna that collects radio waves from space. The signals are sent to a control building, where a computer system analyzes them and in some cases makes a picture of the object that produced them.

Radio telescopes have several advantages over optical telescopes. They can penetrate farther into space and can be used around the clock, rain or shine. This is because radio waves penetrate clouds, and heavenly bodies emit radio signals even in the daytime. Discoveries made with radio telescopes include quasars—

distant galaxies that are powerful radio sources—and the fast-spinning stars called pulsars that were described earlier.

Heavenly bodies aren't the only sources of radio waves. People, too, have transmitted them since Guglielmo Marconi invented radio in 1895. Since about 1929 we have also broadcast television, a type of radio signal. AM radio waves bounce off our atmosphere and return to Earth, but FM radio signals travel forever into space at the speed of light. TV broadcasts use FM radio waves, so they also travel forever into space at 186,282 miles (300,000 kilometers) per second. This means that we have another way to contact extraterrestrials besides visiting them or welcoming them to our planet. We can exchange radio messages.

Beings on a distant world who aimed a radio telescope our way might detect our radio signals, depending on several factors. Since we have broadcast FM radio and TV signals for only about 60 years, their planet would have to be within about 60 light-years of Earth. Also, since the signals can be transmitted over billions of frequencies, the listeners would have to tune to the right channel or station.

If in the year we call 1997, extraterrestrials 40 light-years away point their radio telescopes at Earth and tune in on the right frequencies, they could receive our radio and TV shows from 1957. Broadcasts they might receive include Dwight Eisenhower's second inauguration as president, reports of Russia's launch of *Sputnik I,* and the 1957 World Series between the Milwaukee Braves and the New York Yankees. If the ETs built special receivers and large antenna systems, they could actually watch our TV shows and listen to our FM radio broadcasts. In that case they might become fans of *I Love Lucy* and *The Three Stooges.* But even if the extraterrestrials only detected our signals as static, they would know we're here. Signals sent by intelligent beings are stronger than natural background static. They are also at a specific frequency, whereas natural radio noise from heavenly bodies covers many frequencies at once.

STARTING TO LISTEN

Like us, distant civilizations might also broadcast radio waves. In their landmark article "Searching for Interstellar Communications," published in *Nature*

Theoretically, the TV show I Love Lucy, popular in the 1950s, could be received in the late 1990s by extraterrestrials 40 light-years away. Of course, this would be possible only if they pointed their radio telescopes at Earth and tuned them to just the right frequency.

in 1959, Philip Morrison and Giuseppe Cocconi argued that our radio telescopes should be used to search for such signals. They couldn't guarantee success. Yet, they reasoned, "if we never search, the chance of success is zero."

Their article helped inspire the start of SETI, which refers to the *S*earch for *E*xtra*t*errestrial *I*ntelligence using radio telescopes. The scientific community soon embraced SETI as the most practical way to search for intelligent life beyond Earth.

Astronomer Frank Drake conducted the first SETI project in 1960. Dr. Drake called his search Project Ozma, "named for the princess of the imaginary land of Oz—a place very far away, difficult to reach, and populated by exotic beings," he explained. Project Ozma involved 150 hours of "listening" with the radio

The radio telescope at the National Radio Astronomy Observatory in Green Bank, West Virginia, measures 300 feet (91 meters) in diameter. It was used in the first search for extraterrestrial intelligence (SETI) project in 1960.

telescope at the National Radio Astronomy Observatory in Green Bank, West Virginia. Only two stars were studied—Tau Ceti and Epsilon Eridani—both similar to the Sun. Drake did not detect any alien radio signals.

EXPANDING THE SEARCH

A drawback with Ozma and other early SETI projects was that they could study only one channel at a time. The chances for success would rise if many channels could be monitored at once. By the early 1980s Harvard University physics professor Paul Horowitz had developed Suitcase SETI, a system that could scan

128,000 channels simultaneously and that could be moved about and attached to various radio telescopes.

In 1982 Dr. Horowitz plugged Suitcase SETI into the huge radio telescope at Arecibo Observatory in Puerto Rico. For 75 hours, Horowitz monitored 250 Sun-like stars in search of radio signals sent by intelligent beings. Like Drake, he found none. This was no cause for alarm, for 250 stars are hardly a drop of milk in the Milky Way.

After Suitcase SETI, Horowitz built META (for *Megachannel Extraterrestrial Assay*), a receiver that could study 8.4 million channels at once. In 1985 META began searching for alien signals from its home at the 84-foot (26-meter) Harvard University/Smithsonian radio telescope outside Boston, Massachusetts. Other SETI projects also developed receivers that could analyze thousands to millions of channels simultaneously.

By the early 1990s, more than 60 SETI searches in about 10 countries had been undertaken. No alien messages had been intercepted, yet scientists remained optimistic. They agreed that it might take decades of searching to detect even one signal. Besides, the future seemed bright, for NASA was planning a big SETI project that was to use several radio telescopes.

NASA's SETI search began in 1992. Its yearly budget was $12 million—a tiny amount compared to other government programs. But the hopes of SETI enthusiasts soon came crashing down to Earth. Due to budget cuts Congress withdrew the funds in 1993, ending NASA's newborn program. By 1996 the world's five major SETI projects were all funded by private donations.

SETI TODAY

Astronomer Seth Shostak of the SETI Institute explains how today's SETI projects typically work:

> First astronomers aim their radio telescope at likely targets, such as nearby stars like our Sun which might have planets like Earth. The radio telescope collects cosmic static from that direction. Computers then split up the chunk of the radio dial being studied into many millions of channels. Since SETI researchers can't listen to all

those channels themselves, another computer monitors for them and beeps if any of those channels contains an interesting signal. In that case, the computer produces a diagram of the signal that might look like wavy lines or a mountain range. If one signal sticks up higher than the others, this means it is stronger than the natural static and could be a message from ET. However, further study could show that the signal is only interference from a TV station on Earth or even a microwave oven.

The SETI Institute, an organization based near San Francisco, California, runs Project Phoenix, one of the five current SETI searches. The ancient Greeks believed that a bird called the phoenix lived 500 years, burned itself, then arose newborn from its own ashes. Similarly, Project Phoenix rose from the ashes of NASA's SETI program. Before it ended, that project developed a receiver that can monitor 28 million channels simultaneously. Project Phoenix is using this equipment for a "targeted search" of about a thousand Sunlike stars. Directed by Dr. Jill Tarter, Project Phoenix began in 1995 at the Parkes Radio Telescope in Australia, where 200 Sunlike stars were studied. Dr. Tarter plans to use other radio telescopes in the late 1990s to study 800 more Sunlike stars.

The world's longest-running SETI program, begun in 1974, is conducted at Ohio State University's "Big Ear" Radio Telescope in Delaware, Ohio. Visitors are often puzzled by the flag—showing yellow, blue, and white spheres against a black field—next to Big Ear. "It is the flag of Earth, designed by a man in Illinois, and it flies everywhere a SETI search takes place," explains Dr. Robert S. Dixon, director of Big Ear's SETI program. The spheres represent the Sun, Earth, and Moon, while the black field stands for space. The idea behind the flag is that SETI can help us think globally—"teach us that Earth is a small part of a big universe, that the things we argue and fight wars over are not very important, and that we must learn to cooperate," Dixon says. Of course, finding an alien signal would help achieve this goal.

There are two kinds of extraterrestrial signals a SETI search could detect, according to Dixon. A radio telescope might intercept broadcasts that a civilization intends for its own use but that leak into space as our FM radio and TV broadcasts do. This kind of signal is known as leakage, and the search for it is called eavesdropping, because the senders would not intend to be overheard.

The flag of Earth flies wherever a SETI search takes place. It is shown here next to "Big Ear"— Ohio State University's radio telescope in Delaware, Ohio.

Or, a civilization might send out a message in the hope that it will be intercepted. This type of signal is called a beacon, because the extraterrestrials would be advertising their presence.

"Both kinds of signals could be detected, but it is more likely that a beacon would be discovered because it would tend to be more powerful," Dixon explains.

Another reason, besides its strength, might make a beacon signal easier to detect. To boost their chances of making contact, extraterrestrials might send a message over channels with special mathematical significance—"magic frequencies," SETI scientists call them. These include 1.4 gigahertz (the frequency of neutral hydrogen, the most plentiful element in the universe) and 1.7 gigahertz (the frequency of hydroxyl, which consists of hydrogen and oxygen).

"At Big Ear we study the frequencies between 1.4 and 1.7 gigahertz, which is called the 'water hole' region," says Dixon. The nickname originated because these frequencies are logical places where civilizations might meet to talk, like water holes on a desert, and because neutral hydrogen and hydroxyl together make water.

Dixon also thinks that an alien signal might arrive in the form of a simple math test—"They might send a message that goes *Beep, beep-beep, beep-beep-beep, beep-beep-beep-beep.*" Once the computer alerted them that each set of signals was increasing by one, scientists could actually listen to the beeps and record them.

HIT-AND-RUN SIGNALS

It is a little-known fact that, over the years, SETI projects have scored several "hits"—signals that might be from extraterrestrials but that couldn't be located again. A famous hit received by Big Ear in 1977 from a point in the sky near the center of the Milky Way galaxy is known as the "WOW signal," because the excited technician who found it wrote "Wow!" on the chart. "It was one of the best examples anyone has seen of what might have been an extraterrestrial signal," says Dixon. "But as it came in, it suddenly turned off, like someone had flipped a switch. Perhaps it was a super-secret military satellite transmitting on an illegal frequency, or perhaps it was a signal from an alien civilization or an alien spacecraft. We'll never know."

Dr. Dixon explains: "We don't ever want to claim we've made contact with extraterrestrials and have it turn out to be a false alarm, so everyone conducting searches has signed a SETI Detection Protocol. If we found a likely signal, we would check our equipment carefully to make sure there was no malfunction. Then we would call another SETI scientist like Tarter or Horowitz and ask them to look for the signal with their equipment. If they found it, that would pretty well nail it down."

META AND BETA

Paul Horowitz ran his 8.4-million-channel META search at the 84-foot (26-meter) radio telescope at Harvard, Massachusetts, for ten years. Meanwhile, with finan-

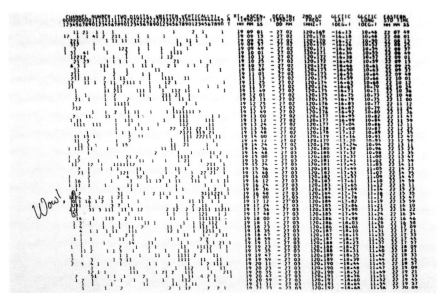

This signal received in 1977 from a point in the sky near the center of the Milky Way caused much excitement, but it turned off suddenly and has never been identified as an attempt by extraterrestrials to contact Earth.

cial help from the Planetary Society, a group interested in space exploration and SETI research, the Harvard University physicist developed his Billion-Channel Extraterrestrial Assay, which can monitor 2 billion radio channels (a quarter of a billion of them at once)—the most of any SETI system on Earth. "This is like having a quarter of a billion radios sitting on your desk, each one tuned to a different channel," Dr. Horowitz explained in 1995 when BETA began operating at the 84-foot radio telescope.

Although BETA is a great improvement over META, 8.4 million channels are nothing to sneeze at, so by 1996 the Planetary Society was looking for a radio telescope that it could hook up to Horowitz's old META system. META also has a twin, META II, which is run by the Argentine Institute of Radio Astronomy in the South American country of Argentina. Of the five current SETI projects, it is the only search now being performed in the Southern Hemisphere, where different stars are visible than in the Northern Hemisphere.

BIG DISH IN PUERTO RICO

The fifth major SETI program is conducted at the world's largest radio-radar telescope, the 1,000-foot (300-meter) dish at Arecibo Observatory in Puerto Rico. Standing near the mammoth dish, radio astronomer Dr. Mike Davis explained that the instrument is needed for various research programs and can't focus only on SETI. Scientists have found a way around this by installing a SETI system at Arecibo that, in Davis's words, "rides piggyback" on other astronomical projects. Whenever the instrument studies natural radio emissions, it also searches for signals from extraterrestrials.

The Arecibo program is called Project Serendip—from the word *serendipity,* which means finding something valuable while not searching for it directly. Scientists hope that Project Serendip will detect a message from aliens as the radio telescope does other astronomical research.

The large radio telescope at Arecibo is situated in a natural crater in the mountains of Puerto Rico. It is used for a number of astronomical projects.

THE MANY-EYED MONSTER

Anyone who has lost a ball in a field of weeds or dropped a key on the way home from school knows that the missing object can sometimes be found quickly but often requires a thorough search. SETI is a little like that. So far we have examined only a tiny portion of the universe in search of alien radio signals. Assuming there are signals to be detected, we may have to make more thorough searches for many years before discovering an extraterrestrial message.

Most people don't get excited about research that probably won't pay off during their lifetimes, which is why SETI programs tend to suffer from a shortage of funds and sometimes a lack of interest. A sad example of this is occurring at the Big Ear Radio Telescope, which may be dismantled in the late 1990s. The owner of the land has sold the property to a developer who wants to build houses on the site and enlarge an adjoining golf course.

Undaunted by the possible end of the world's longest-running SETI project, Dr. Robert Dixon plans to continue his work because, as he says, "SETI is *so* important!" In fact, he is working on a new project that could be the most momentous event in the history of SETI. It will be called Argus, named for the 100-eyed monster in Greek mythology who could see in all directions.

A problem with today's radio telescopes is that they study only one place in the sky at a time, Dixon explains. We might not notice a beacon if we aren't pointing a radio telescope at the right spot when the signal arrives. "Argus will look in all directions all the time," says Dixon. "It will be composed of a hundred thousand or even a million small antennas that together will scan the whole sky in all directions continuously." Hooked up to the antennas will be an even larger number of small computers that will process the information. Dixon and his colleagues have built a prototype, or model, of Argus, consisting of a few antennas. "We hope to have the big Argus going in ten years," says Dixon, which would be in about the year 2007.

What makes Argus especially exciting is that the public will be able to take part in it. "Argus will be on the Internet computer network," continues Dixon. "Anyone on Earth whose computer is also hooked up to the Internet could study any part of the sky they wanted." The public could actually tap into the radio

With proper Internet training, students could be a part of future SETI projects.

data as it comes in. A sixth-grade student, for example, could become involved in SETI as a hobby and discover an extraterrestrial message at virtually the same time that Argus's central computer locates the signal.

Five offers of free land have already been made for the project, but building Argus will be costly. Dixon is trying to obtain funds from such sources as the National Science Foundation, NASA, the SETI Institute, and the Planetary Society.

Even Argus would have limitations. For one thing, a growing amount of radio frequency interference (RFI) is assaulting our planet's radio telescopes. These are not the "hits" like the WOW signal that might actually be extraterrestrial messages. RFI refers to "human noise" from such sources as cellular phones, police radar, and aircraft communications equipment. Another limitation of Earth-based radio telescopes is that our planet blocks out half the sky at any given time.

SETI scientists have thought of ways to solve these problems. Radio frequency interference could be avoided by building a SETI observatory on the far side of the Moon. However, as on Earth, the Moon would block out much of the sky at any given moment. Another idea is to launch a SETI radio telescope into orbit around Earth. Such an instrument would not only be beyond most RFI; it could scan the entire sky. "An Argus system in space would be the ultimate monitoring system," says Dixon. "We could listen to everything in every direction in the universe all the time." Dixon predicts that in about 2017, the United States or another nation will launch an orbiting SETI observatory, which he has nicknamed "Earthpost."

ANSWERING THE CALL

One day radio astronomers may intercept a signal from afar that doesn't seem natural. They will check and recheck to make sure it isn't coming from Earth or caused by a defect in their equipment. If another radio telescope verifies that the message is of alien origin, there will be a historic news bulletin: WE ARE NOT ALONE!

The discovery of an extraterrestrial message would create tremendously exciting possibilities, to say the least. Assuming that we have built starships by that time, we might send an expedition to visit our cosmic correspondents. If we informed them of our whereabouts, they might send an expedition to visit us. Or, we could become long-distance pen pals—more properly, radio pals—with the extraterrestrials.

If the aliens were 50 light-years away, each side of a conversation would require 50 years to travel through space. We might spend centuries just trying to decipher each other's language. Once we did that, we might send them an encyclopedia of our knowledge, and they might do the same for us, so that we could learn about one another. The information we would gain from the extraterrestrials would be worth the wait between each side of the conversation, say SETI enthusiasts. Yet there are those who warn that, should we ever intercept an alien message, we should not let them know we're here at all.

7

What If . . . ?

The finding of intelligent life beyond Earth would be the most profound discovery in history.

—Physicist Dr. Daniel P. Whitmire

What if in 2020 radio astronomers detect a message from a distant civilization? What if in 2030 an extraterrestrial spaceship lands on the White House lawn, or if in 2288 astronauts discover an inhabited planet? Any of these events would have an impact comparable to Copernicus's discovery that Earth is not the center of the universe, says SETI researcher Dr. Jill Tarter. Stories about the aliens would dominate the news for months, perhaps years, and teachers and religious leaders would attempt to convey the significance of the breakthrough.

Some people would take the news in stride. "I wouldn't be surprised if we detected an alien radio signal because I believe in extraterrestrials," said Clyde Tombaugh, the discoverer of Pluto. Other people would probably be disturbed to learn that the universe is not ours alone. Meanwhile, politicians and scientists might argue over who should speak to the aliens first, and military leaders would probably warn that we must be prepared to fight them.

The most valuable people at first could be communications experts. If we met the extraterrestrials in person, and if they had something akin to eyes and hands, we might use sign language to begin a dialogue with them, much as Native Americans used long ago and deaf people use today. Assuming the aliens have something akin to ears and mouths, we might learn each other's languages by pointing to things, saying the words for them, and listening to their responses.

Even if there is no personal contact, there are ways to understand each other with radio messages. We could exchange radio signals that when processed by computers would form various pictures. We might begin by exchanging information about mathematics, later learn each other's alphabets, and eventually communicate in sentences. "For just a few hundred dollars we could transmit the entire *Encyclopaedia Britannica* to them," figures Arecibo Observatory's Dr. Mike Davis, although by the time the encyclopedia arrived it might be hundreds of years old.

CONCERNS RAISED BY CONTACT

Not everyone is convinced that a dialogue with extraterrestrials would be wise. "Potentially there is a lot we can gain from beings who might be as far ahead of us as we are [ahead of] earthworms," says University of Tennessee astronomer Dr. Mark Littmann. "Yet they might be so superior to us that it would put an end to human endeavor. Why should we try to gain new knowledge and make new discoveries if all we have to do is tap into their knowledge?"

It is also possible that the aliens would try to conquer or enslave us, as depicted in a number of flying saucer movies. The Czechoslovakian-born astronomer Zdenek Kopal has issued a dire warning about this. "Should we ever hear the space-phone ringing, for God's sake let us not answer, but rather make ourselves as inconspicuous as possible to avoid attracting attention," he has cautioned. Otherwise, claims Professor Kopal, "We might find ourselves in their test tubes or other contraptions set up to investigate us, as we investigate insects or guinea pigs."

Radio astronomers Robert Dixon and Mike Davis respond that it is too late to follow this advice. "We can't hide our existence," says Dr. Dixon. "We've been sending out FM radio and TV signals for more than 50 years." Dr. Davis points out that, in addition to leakage from our radio and TV broadcasts, Earthlings have beamed a radio message through space. It was done in 1974 using Arecibo Observatory's powerful radar. When converted to a picture by a computer, the message would show our counting system, our Sun and nine planets, as well as images of a person and of the Arecibo Radio Telescope. As of 1997 the message, which moves at the speed of light, had traveled 23 light-years from Earth.

In fact, many people think that aliens would have more to fear from us than we would from them. We have often killed or enslaved our fellow human be-

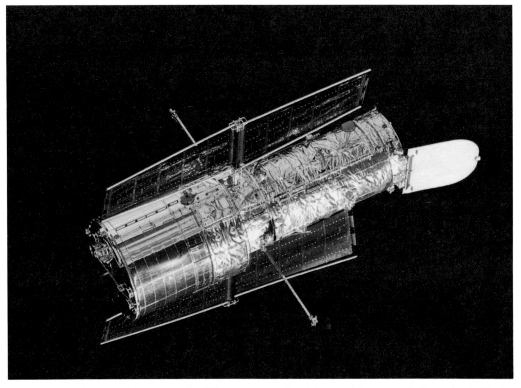

The Hubble Space Telescope (HST) *was launched into orbit around Earth in 1990. Its flawed optics were repaired in 1993, and it is shown here just after astronauts walked in space to service it again in early 1997. At 375 miles (600 kilometers) above Earth, it is our eye on the universe, probing deep space in the continuing search for other worlds and clues to the beginning of the universe.*

ings. If we are so cruel to other people, how might we treat beings who seem totally different from us?

Extraterrestrials and humans probably should be wary of each other. Before exchanging information we might make a peace treaty, as countries on Earth do to prevent hostilities. But our natural curiosity would make it nearly impossible for us to ignore the "space-phone," for who could resist trying to find out about the callers?

Besides, most SETI researchers insist, the dangers of contact would almost certainly be outweighed by the benefits, which might include our very survival. Fifty years after inventing radio, Earthlings created nuclear bombs, which have the potential to destroy civilization. Extraterrestrials also might have developed nuclear weapons soon after inventing radio. What if civilizations tend to destroy themselves with nuclear devices soon after entering the "communicative phase," as SETI scientists call the radio age?

"If we detect intelligence on another planet, it would prove that at least one other civilization lasted long enough for us to receive their signal," says Dr. Mike Davis. "That would be extremely encouraging." Project Phoenix director Dr. Jill Tarter adds: "If anyone is out there for us to discover, they must be long-term survivors. Finding them will tell us that it is possible for us to survive our technological infancy." The extraterrestrials might even share the secret of world peace with us, as Percival Lowell hoped the Martians would do.

Aliens who are far more advanced than we are could help us in many other ways. They might teach us how to conquer cancer and other diseases, and how to clean up our planet and feed everyone who lives on it. "The possibilities of what we could learn from them are unlimited," says Dr. Daniel Whitmire. "We might learn the secret of immortality, or how to build better spaceships." In short, from a few hours of reading their encyclopedia or meeting with them, we might gather knowledge that would take us a million years to discover on our own.

MIND-BLOWING POSSIBILITIES

"It may turn out that the universe is teeming with life, and that every star has signals sent to it by intelligent beings," says Arecibo Observatory's Mike Davis.

He and most other scientists think that we will probably discover extraterrestrial intelligence one day. However, we cannot rule out another possibility.

"Maybe it's dead quiet out there, and there is no one else besides us," continues Davis. "If we keep doing SETI searches, and if we keep making improvements such as increasing the number of channels, then eventually we'll be doing much more sensitive searches compared to today. And if hundreds of years pass and we don't detect a signal, it would gradually sink in that we may be alone. Yet finding that out could be just as important as making contact. Many people are terribly disappointed at how we're polluting our planet. If we knew we were alone, we might realize that Earth is a unique and very fragile place in space and do more to protect it. And perhaps we would realize that life is very precious and do more to cherish it."

The search for extraterrestrial intelligence is one of the most important scientific quests humans have ever attempted. It is also one of the few in which either answer is exciting. As SETI researcher Dr. Paul Horowitz of Harvard University says: "Either intelligent life exists in other places beyond Earth or we are alone in the universe. Either possibility is mind-blowing, isn't it?"

Numbers, Measures, and Conversions

one hundred = 100

one thousand = 1,000

one hundred thousand = 100,000

one million = 1,000,000

one billion = 1,000,000,000

one trillion = 1,000,000,000,000

one quadrillion = 1,000,000,000,000,000

one sextillion = 1,000,000,000,000,000,000,000

one tredecillion = 1,000,000,000,000,000,000,000,000,000,000,000,000,000,000,000

millisecond = one thousandth of a second

speed of light = 186,282 miles per second; about 300,000 kilometers per second

speed of radio waves = the same as the speed of light

light-year = the distance light travels in a year—5,880,000,000,000 (5.88 trillion) miles, about 9.5 trillion kilometers

F = abbreviation for Fahrenheit, a temperature scale in which 32°F is the freezing point of water and 212°F is the boiling point of water

C = abbreviation for Celsius, a temperature scale in which 0°C is the freezing point of water and 100°C is the boiling point of water

To convert Fahrenheit (F) to Celsius (C), subtract 32 degrees from the Fahrenheit temperature, then multiply the remainder by $\frac{5}{9}$.

To convert Celsius to Fahrenheit, multiply the Celsius temperature by $\frac{9}{5}$, then add 32 degrees to the product.

To convert miles to kilometers, multiply the miles by 1.6.

To convert feet to meters, multiply the feet by 0.3.

For Further Information

BOOKS

Bryan, C.D.B. *Close Encounters of the Fourth Kind: A Reporter's Notebook on Alien Abduction, UFOs, and the Conference at M.I.T.* New York: Penguin Arkana, 1996.

Canadeo, Anne. *UFOs: The Fact or Fiction Files.* New York: Walker, 1990.

Darling, David. *Could You Ever Fly to the Stars?* Minneapolis: Dillon Press, 1990.

Deem, James M. *How to Catch a Flying Saucer.* Boston: Houghton Mifflin, 1991.

Gallant, Roy A. *Beyond Earth: The Search for Extraterrestrial Life.* New York: Four Winds Press, 1977.

Herbst, Judith. *Star Crossing: How to Get Around in the Universe.* New York: Atheneum, 1993.

Koppeschaar, Carl. *Moon Handbook: A 21st-Century Travel Guide.* Chico, Calif.: Moon Publications, 1995.

Mallove, Eugene F., and Gregory L. Matloff. *The Starflight Handbook: A Pioneer's Guide to Interstellar Travel.* New York: Wiley, 1989.

McDonough, Thomas R. *The Search for Extraterrestrial Intelligence: Listening for Life in the Cosmos.* New York: Wiley, 1987.

Nardo, Don. *Flying Saucers: Opposing Viewpoints.* San Diego: Greenhaven Press, 1996.

Sullivan, Walter. *We Are Not Alone: The Continuing Search for Extraterrestrial Intelligence.* Rev. ed. New York: Dutton, 1993.

White, Frank. *The SETI Factor.* New York: Walker, 1990.

CD-ROM

Eyewitness Encyclopedia of Space and the Universe. DK Multimedia. 1996. Windows. $39.95. Grade 4 up.

Invisible Universe. Voyager. 1996. Mac. $39.95. Grade 9 up.

Index

References to illustrations are in **bold**, *italic* type.

abduction by UFOs, 53–54
Aldrin, Edwin "Buzz," 18
Andromeda galaxy, 36, 40
antimatter, 44
Apollo II, 18
Arecibo Radio Telescope, 28, 60, **65**, 65, 70
Argus, 66
Armstrong, Neil, 18
astronauts, 18, 37–38
atoms, 43

beacon signals, 62
BETA (Billion-Channel Extraterrestrial Assay), 9, 64
"Big Ear" Radio Telescope, 61, **62**, 63, 66
Butler, Paul, 30–31

Cassini, 22
Cocconi, Giuseppe, 58

Cochran, William, 31
colonies in space, 38–40
communicating with extraterrestrials, 69–70
contact with extraterrestrials, 72, 70
Copernicus, Nicolaus, 12
"cosmic speed limit," 40, 42

Davis, Dr. Mike, 33, 65, 70, 72, 73
de Bergerac, Cyrano, *11*, 11
Dixon, Dr. Robert S., 61, 66, 70
Drake, Frank, 58

Earth, 12, 21
"Earthpost," 68
"eavesdropping," 61
Einstein, Albert, 42
electrons, 44
Europa, *22*, 22

flag of Earth, 61, *62*
flying saucers, 48

galaxies, 27
Galilei, Galileo, 12, *13*, 26
Galileo, 19, ***22***, 22
Goddard, Robert, 16, *17*
gravity, 12, 28

Hershel, William, 12
Hill, Barney and Betty, 53
Hipparchus, 10
Horowitz, Dr. Paul, 9, 58, 59, 63, 73
Hubble Space Telescope (HST), ***20***, 27, ***71***
humanoids, 53
Hynek, J. Allen, 54–55

internet, 66–67
interstellar ramjet, 43–44
ion-propulsion spaceship, 44

Jupiter, 12, 19, 22

Kepler, Johannes, 11

leakage signals, 61, 71
light years, 36
Lowell, Percival, 14
Lucian, 10
Lucid, Shannon, *39*

Magellan, 19
"magic frequencies," 62
Marconi, Guglielmo, 14, 57
Marcy, Geoffrey, 30–31
Mariner 10, 19
Mars, 12, 13, 14, 15, 19, 23, 24–25, 37

Mars Global Surveyor, 24
Marsokhod, *41*
Mars Pathfinder, 24, *25*
Mars Sample Return Mission, 24
Mayor, Michel, 30
Mercury, 12, 19
META (Megachannel Extraterrestrial Assay) and META II, 59–60, 63, 64
microfossils, 23, *24*
the Milky Way, 12, 26
Miller, Stanley, 33
millisecond pulsars, 28
Mir, *39*
the Moon, 10, 13, 18
Morrison, Philip, 58
movies about extraterrestrials, 15

NASA, 21, 23, 24, 32
National Astronomy Observatory radio telescope, *59*, 59
Neptune, 12, *20*, 20, 21
Newton, Isaac, 12

orbit, 21, 28–30
origins of intelligent life, 33–34

Planet Finder, 32, 37
planets, 27–32
Planet X, 21
plasma, 43
Pluto, 12, 20–21
positron, 44
Powell, Dr. Conley, 21, 33, 37, 43, 44
Project Ozma, 58–59
Project Phoenix, 61

Project Serendip, 65
Proxima Centauri, 36, 42
pulsars, 28, 29

quasars, 56–57
Queloz, Didier, 30

radio frequency interference (RFI), 67, 68
radio signals, 14, 57
radio telescopes, 28, *29*, 56, *59*
Reber, Grote, 56
"Rip Van Winkle technique," 37–38
robots, interstellar travel by, 37
rockets, 16, 43, 44

Saturn, 12, 21
Schiaparelli, Giovanni, 14
SETI (Search for Extraterrestrial Intelligence), 58–68
SETI Detection Protocol, 63
Shepard, Alan, 16
Sirus, *36*
the solar system, 12
spacecraft, 42–45. *See also* rockets
space probes, 18, 19
spectrograph, 30
spectrometer, *31*
spectrum, 30
Sputnick I, 16, *17*, 57

stars, 12, 26–31
stories about extraterrestrials, 11, 12
Suitcase SETI, 59–60
the Sun, 12, 13, 28

television signals, 57, *58*, 70
theory of relativity, 42, 45
"time dilation," 45–46
Titan, 21
Todd, David, 14
Tombaugh, Clyde, 20, 21, 34, 42, 69
travel, interstellar, 35–42

UFOs (unidentified flying objects), 47–56
Uranus, 12, 19–20, 21
Urey, Harold, 33

Van Flandern, Tom, 21
Venus, 12, 13, 19, 37
Viking I and *Viking II*, 19, 23
Voltaire, 12
Voyager 1 and *Voyager 2*, 19, 35, *36*, 36

Wan Hu, 9, 10, *10*
"water hole region," 63
Wells, H.G., 14, *15*
Wolszczan, Alex, 28, 29
"WOW signal," 63, *64*, 67